21 Days

A poetic journey from Singapore to Malaysia
in September 2019

Published in Great Britain in 2021
by Big White Shed, Nottingham
www.bigwhiteshed.co.uk
Printed and bound by Ben's Books, UK & Totem, Poland

ISBN 978-1-9163105-8-2
Copyright © Christopher Towers
Cover & illustration by Raphael Achache

A CIP catalogue record of this book is available
from the British Library.

To Cynthia

CONTENTS

Setting the Scene

This collection of poems reflects experiences on a holiday to Singapore and Malaysia in the September of 2019. I precede each poem with some broader thoughts and recollections. These reflections are of only two or three lines, to whet the appetite and set the scene. I want the poems to 'speak'.

The poems tell stories of people and places met and discovered, from the arrival at the V Lavender Hotel to the departure from Changi airport, twenty-one days later. I started writing my diary from the outset after buying and using a note pad to reflect my thoughts from each day. These were talking about the grandeur of a hotel to the apparent poverty of a woman dissecting the contents of a rubbish bin in *By the Kallang River*. The work reflects some wider issues as I pondered the dramatic happenings in the UK Parliament as my 'home' country grappled with leaving the European Union. The world continued to change, with anxieties around free movement of people and national identities. Some of the poems reflect upon these political changes from stories of 'foreign' care workers waiting to secure care work, to thoughts on issues of ageing and family ties.

The poems are written in first person and reflect concerns and uncertainties and on other occasions provide commentary on buildings, places and spaces from the Singapore National Stadium to the causeway to Malaysia, and Arab Street. I also reflect on the personal, with poems such as *Chin Swee Road*. This was based upon my wife's aunt and her life experiences as I engaged in a conversation with her in her flat, to *Smiles Through Her Laksa* about my wife and her mother and the yearnings of time and distance. All the poems are 'free verse', a deliberate choice, in order to tell a story or stories free from the potential constraints of rhyme or other structures.

DAY 1

Sunday, September 1

That familiar sense of disorientation whirled around my head upon arrival at Changi Airport. Arriving at the hotel I noticed how palatial it looked. My eyes strained under bright lights but my tiredness from the flight was somewhat dissipated by my adrenaline at being the other side of the world.

Arriving at the V Lavender Hotel

Concierge, in brown and gold tunic,
smiled with servitude.
Hands together, as if in prayer.

I, like Raffles, straight
from a London plane, dazzling under
chandeliers, arrived at the V Lavender.

Carrying privilege without knowing,
treading a floor, glistening.
I smelt kaya toast from nearby cafes

drifting through the opulent spaces
with shining panels and paintings that
old colonists may have valued.

A gold-plated lift carried me
to floor eight, below the swimming pool,
where men in bath robes sauntered,

holding isolated smiles,
with open toed sandals on soft carpets,
fragrant with the smell of orchids by the bay.

Fresh linen awaited, its softness
to touch expectant skin, its pleasures
unfolding, softly, before me, as if a birth right.

DAY 2

Monday, September 2

We decided to go for a run by the local river. Accustomed to running on soft ground in England, there was a strange sense of the familiar in the spacious grass fields by the water. We crossed the busy highway to get there, festooned with cars racing around as if the Grand Prix, due in the city later in the month, had already arrived.

By the Kallang River

I saw her as I wandered by
the Kallang River,
far from the opaque
endless shopping malls
of plenitude.

She scavenged
with forked fingers,
plucking and picking
at scraps from the
waste bins.

Shovelling empties of
Coca-Cola bottles into bags
with all the tenacity
of a hungry bird,
pecking and poking.

I could see skyscrapers
with glories and stories
of a country transformed.
Eating opulence.

Meanwhile she devoured the garbage,
like a cynomolgus monkey,
feeding on the left behinds
of a feast.

DAY 3

Tuesday, September 3

Day three arrived and we went to stay at the YMCA. This was very different from the V Lavender Hotel. That was opulent, this was basic. But we intended to stay there for the rest of the three weeks, apart from a visit to Malaysia in the middle of the trip.

Upon Fort Canning

I ran upon Fort Canning,
as hot as a kiln,
perspiring in an
equatorial furnace.

The Malays called it
the forbidden hill
where the kings of
ancient Singapore

were laid to rest,
left to haunt
those that came later,
like the colonists,

who hoisted the
union jack
upon this hallowed
space.

Knots of foliage buzzed
with intensity,
as threads of sweat
fell to my chest.

DAY 4

Wednesday, September 4

I always like to see and hear the side of a country not written of too much, but known only to those that experience it directly. Singapore was and is the country of my wife's birth and she knows it as an insider. I could never see it as she does.

Waiting

They waited, maids,
at the employment agency,
hands locked,
tense.

Soon,
to touch skin of others,
pressing flesh on flesh
not known to them,

to support shoulders
with their hands,
touch hips and
unsettle emotions.

To swap the dollar
for their labour,
no gifts,
just exchange.

Their own intimacies
put on hold,
their dreams
mothballed.

DAY 5

Thursday, September 5

It was always my intention to see some sport in the country and a World Cup Qualifier fitted the bill. Football is not 'big' in this country but that was irrelevant. I wanted to see and hear how a game so familiar to me in England 'looked' here.

To the National Stadium
(Singapore v Yemen, World Cup Qualifier)

I saw Indian workers
with sullen half smiles.
Eyes sunken, morose.
They lined old jeeps,
rattling on roads.

Their blue overalls
mottled with mud or oil.
Human cargo, scarred,
counting ringgits
for dollars.

Back to their lodgings
as the spangled lights
of the National Stadium
glistened
under moist skies.

I heard the cry 'Singapura'.
It rang around the train.
Half modest, half proud,
as the Indians
rolled on home.

DAY 6

Friday, September 6

My wife longed to see her mother and it was palpably clear with the knowing looks between them, that the bond was tight. All I could do was observe in quiet desperation, unable to offer a bridge between or compensate for the chasm that time and distance appeared to create.

Smiles Through Her Laksa

She smiled from behind her laksa bowl,
in shy reverence, at her mother,
glimpsed through the clutter of the table.

The soy sauce bottle jostled with
saucers, bowls and extra spoons.
I just wished I could do more

than observe their mutual longings,
expressed no more than once a month,
behind a computer screen, when time allows.

DAY 7

Saturday, September 7

We walked through the endless eateries on busy streets and came to an ex-convent school for girls converted into a restaurant. It was a short distance from our rooms at the YMCA. I noticed a plaque on the wall. It was a place where unwanted babies were left by mothers for nuns to take in.

Chijmes

And in this place,
the Chijmes,
where nuns walked
through gates of hope
and convent girls
graced the arches,

restaurants
heaved
with smells of fish oil,
infused chilli
and steamed rice,
cooked in hot kitchens.

The brilliance
of marriage gowns
shone in white,
trading freedom
for loving ties,

taken to spaces
by familiar
yet strange
partners

known,
but not known.
And in these same
places,
distant cries from
nearby bars, cheered

football teams
from Manchester
and London,

teams familiar
yet foreign.
But like loyal
servants,
they smiled and
cheered the same,

as if independence
never happened.

DAY 8

Sunday, September 8

Clutching the radio to my ear in the quiet of a hotel bedroom I felt like a small boy again, listening to sounds from far away. The voices and tones familiar to me and yet so distant.

Home Thoughts

I listened to
the World Service.
A jewel from the skies,
of Reithian dialects.

A sound to comfort
as much as the soft pillows
resting my head.

I cupped the radio
to the ear for more
as the sky blazed

with scarlet hues
and whiskers of
pink.

I heard tales
from a lost
homeland.

They were closing
Parliament.
England imploded
far, far away.

Sadness,
yearnings,
from a distant post.

DAY 9

Monday, September 9

We went to see Cynthia's mother and family in her flat in Hougang, one of the districts of the city. The flat was fairly high in the block and there was the semblance of a wind.

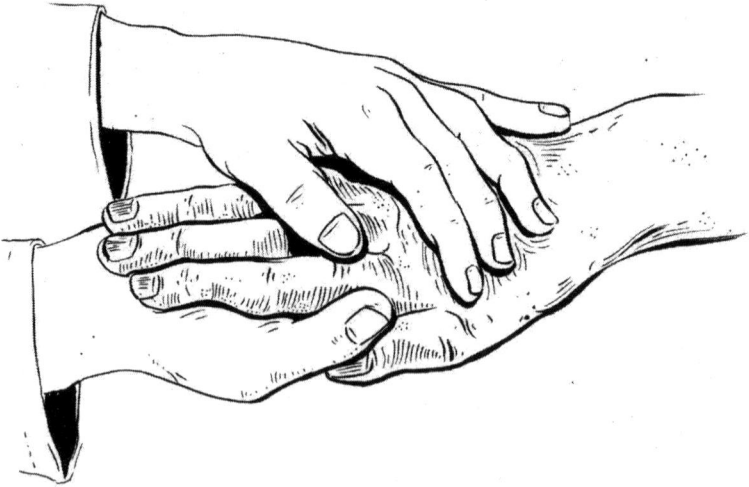

Near Buangkok Green

A kaya bun
provided comfort
as you picked
the sweet dough,
sitting on a bench
on the void deck
near your flat,
as you looked over
the highway,
at the Institute near
Buangkok Green,
a place for the
so-called
mentally ill.

I thought of
social workers
tending souls
of those
who played
upon this void deck
as children,
the other side of
so-called sanity.

You laid your hand
upon my hand.,
resting on a seat
in a communal space
near your home,

near the
swaying trees,
near Buangkok Green.

You asked me if the
rain trees
provided comfort
for the troubled,

or if a simple hand,
laid upon a shoulder
provided solace
for those
over the bridge,
at the Institute,
near Buangkok Green.

DAY 10

Tuesday, September 10

The tour bus that took us to Malacca was sluggish but reliable. The smog from the burning of forests in Indonesia swirled all around the coach park, just the other side of the causeway between Singapore and Malaysia.

Crossing the Causeway

We crawled over the border,
our coach creeping
like a cockroach
on a skirting board,
over the Causeway,
beyond the wire fences
as we headed to Malaysia
from Singapore,

flanked by lines of
trees to plantations
once rich in
palm oil and rubber.
The big wheels
of the coach
stopped in the dusk,
at a service station.

I smelt diesel,
saw ice cream sellers
fighting clusters of
flies.
They stuck
to their trolleys
as dirt from the wagons
mixed with smoke and ash,

swirling above,
from burning
Indonesian forests
shrouding us

as birds
took to flight.

I asked you if you
felt alright
and if your chest
was as tight as mine,

in a forbidding
landscape
that seemed to close
in on us.

DAY 11

Wednesday, September 11

Arriving in Malacca filled me with a sense of calm. All I wanted to do was walk very slowly by the river, which drew me with its snaking heaviness, offset with the serenity of a path winding its way as we headed to a hotel for a light lunch.

The Malacca River

The olive tinted waters, heavy with offal,
slapping in slow whip motion against the river walls,
consumed my eager eyes.

Even the currents that moved cargos
of the spaghetti of sewage, left over from boat houses,
made me smile.

The smells of rotten food, from forgotten buffets,
cabbage and pungent vinegars, invading my air space,
never lessened my sense of peace,

as we walked along the Malacca river from the
hustle of Jonker Street and its fragrant street stalls
to little India, in the sun.

DAY 12

Thursday, September 12

'Going back' always stirs up emotion. This was my first return to Malacca for eight years when I visited with my then wife to be, Cynthia. I recall revelling in the architecture, the terracotta roofed two tier houses and the winding Jonker Street.

Changing

Malacca has changed you said,
as you stood outside Christchurch,
with its red stone and archways,
waiting for the faithful to come.

This town is different you muttered,
watching rickshaws plated gold,
shuttling lovers, two by two,
nudging cars around the square.

I could sense your sadness at
the changing times, speaking
with regret of fewer white buildings,
parting gifts from the Dutch.

You stood outside the Hard-Rock Café,
nibbling pineapple tarts,
asking me,

to not let the treasures in my eyes
turn to stone.

Meanwhile, couples
rode their rickshaws,
with memories
captured in sepia.

DAY 13

Friday, September 13

We spent the day searching for gifts. I spent time on my own musing at carvings and clocks, art and jewellery. Suddenly I saw a reptilian creature under the grates in one of the streets.

The Monitor Lizard

I saw her
in Jonker Walk.
She caught
my eye,
moving slowly
as the world
hurried.

Under the grate,
the lizard,
lithe with scales
and muscled
armour.
I saw her
swimming

where tourists
carried
hungry smiles
for ice kachang,
spending ringgits
with loving
haste.

The lizard moved,
sleek and silent,
from the river
to the town
looking for eggs,
fish and fruit,

as people
searched the streets
passing vendors,
as the lizard
left the lanes.

DAY 14

Saturday, September 14

I felt sadness leaving Malacca and running around the square near the Hatten Hotel in the early hours of the last day in Malaysia.

Leaving Malacca

The sun rose,
the sky making her colours luminous,

shining tints of yellow
upon terracotta roof tops.

Rinsing her decorous paint
in the river of the town.

The sky so clear we could see the Straits
and the tankers shipping oil,

as we peeped through the windows
of the Hatten hotel.

My head still heaving with dreams,
like clothes heavy on washing lines,

as torpedoed light
made its way to the harbour,

and with sublime precision
settled on the mosque.

And as Malacca woke.
we prepared to leave,

taking sadness with us.

DAY 15

Sunday, September 15

We were back in Singapore, and back to the hawker centre as we ate with the family. These centres are part of the heritage of the country and I felt honoured to be part of it.

The Hawker Centre

I saw them with hot woks and
slack wrists, throwing noodles,
flipping roti prata,

preparing chicken rice.
The hawker centre
rattled with words and smiles.

I smelt the long simmering broths
of fish head soup warming
watered floors, forever damp.

Tissues left on chairs to reserve
tables amid the tippy tap of spoons
and plastic sticks on china.

DAY 16

Monday, September 16

The cosmopolitan grandeur of this one city state was never more apparent as the Grand Prix descended. The boards were up and the race-track prepared. We walked behind boards each day as the feeling of anticipation was palpable.

Waiting for the Grand Prix

The boards were up
for the race,
smoke rose,
the thunder was coming.

Toys for the rich,
high octane cars.
The smell of petrol,
smoke and haze,

mixed with magnolia,
and perfume scents.
I smelt sweetness
with diesel

as we waited
for the playboys
to race for garlands
at Marina Bay.

DAY 17

Tuesday, September 17

Cynthia's aunt lived in a poorer area of the city where dense tower blocks stood beside bustling shops selling cut price household items and bags of local snacks, jumbled with a certain care.

Chin Swee Road

Her aunt mixed
a vegetarian bee hoon,
cooked with tenderness,

before sharing photos,
of the man she loved,
from palm to palm.

Her tears hanging,
threads from tear ducts,
then falling

down cheeks,
shining with pride.
She adored the man.

Her words, gentle
as the tick of the clock.
Her love,

as tender as the sun
with its honey rays,
casting light on images,

bright as her eyes,
as the wind
blew from Clark Quay,

drifting through the window
of her flat, on floor 15
Chin Swee Road.

DAY 18

Wednesday, September 18

The light was fading as we approached the district of Bishan but unlike in England the light seems to fade more slowly in the evening, or at least that was my perception.

By the Lamps

Irregular lanterns
like tower blocks
shone over Bishan,
night lights to stars,

looking like knife racks,
made of lego bricks,
ladders to the skies,
but zigzagging.

You smiled obliquely
in a place where a
a huge cemetery for
the Chinese once stood.

Darkness descended
as my mood darkened
with the idea of
leaving Singapore.

I felt sadness
as the lamps
grew brighter in
dissipating light.

DAY 19

Thursday, September 19

We took some time in Arab Street, a curious area, dominated by a huge mosque standing alongside many narrow lanes with all sorts of sellers.

Remembering Arab Street

I'll remember
salmon-coloured slates,
of walkways peppered,
with racks of sliced fish,
prayer rugs and silken scarves.

I'll recall,
smells of jasmine,
curried fish and
the sound of holy prayers
from the mosque.

I'll look back,
when I'm scuffing
snow under silver
skies of an English
winter. Seven
thousand miles from
Arab Street.

DAY 20

Friday, September 20

We went to 'Bar Rouge' for the final night and Cynthia met her long-standing friend there. They knew the place, far above the Grand Prix track that was burning with motor racing cars down below. I was focusing on the glimpses of cars and the interaction between two dear friends of many years.

Bar Rouge

A feeling of time
closing in,
amid the dark
and neon red
of a bar.

In Raffles City,
high above
where the
racing cars
purred on
rubber tyres,
hot.

With scarlet
bar stools and
sofas of soft leather.
Wallets fluttered
with plastic cards,
couples cavorting
with vice.

As we sat, edgy.
Leaving
Singapore
in the morning.
Making the ice
last in the glass,
if time allowed.

We rose from
sumptuous seats
and greeted the lift
with resignation.

We moved.
Seventy-one floors.
Arrived at ground level,
exchanged glances
with her old
time friend
held tears,

and walked away.

DAY 21

Saturday, September 21

Departures are never easy and this one seemed harder than many others. The closeness to my wife's country and her family was felt more keenly than before. It was hard to leave.

Departure

We checked the flight path,
smelt the orchids,
digested the kaya toast.

Binned the paper,
glanced the watch,
finished the teh tarik.

Tagged the bag,
checked the passport,
removed the odour spray.

Binned the liquids,
grabbed the rucksack,
went through the body scan.

Boarded the plane,
with smiling stewards,
lipstick gloss by cheek.

Secured the seatbelt,
slid the backrest,
closed the eyes to dream,

of the Kallang River
and the Chin Swee Road
and the winds from Clark Quay.

Postscript: final thoughts

These twenty-one days were a poetic journey in so many ways, and I left with the same mix of emotion as when I had arrived in Singapore; something, or some part of me left overseas. The days dwindled and I felt increasing sadness at leaving, reflected in more than one of the poems. I have been to the country four times, but this time meant the most.

Listening to the World Service at night was, as much as anything, for the delight at hearing of happenings in England from less than partisan journalists, just pleased to practice their craft. 'Home', at the forefront of my mind. The visit to Malacca provided contrast, much more visceral in a sense, the landscape slightly forbidding. I felt much further away from England when in Malaysia, but that was also exciting, with its slight edge.

The relationship between people and places always intrigues me. I felt closeness to Singapore through the connection of family. It is more 'place' than geographical space because of my relationship to the people. Here I am, writing in England's early spring, yearning to return to Singapore, at some point beyond the end of the pandemic. The country appeals yet more and the yearning to be in another place, far from what I know, ever stronger.

About the Author

Dr Chris Towers is an innovative lecturer by day, who uses drama, film and words to support student learning. He brings poetry into the classroom in ways that supported his winning of a major teaching award. By night he focuses on poetic expression and composes poems that draw from a lifetime of influences from working with vulnerable adults to composing poems for German and Russian students when teaching overseas. He has honed his poetic craft and developed his awareness of poetry and how to work with it in the classroom through post-graduate study at Nottingham Trent and Cambridge University. It is however his life and work experiences including travel that are particularly significant and provide the fuel for his ideas.